Let us Change the World

Geneva S. Rivers

ISBN: 979-8-88615-306-4 (Paperback)

979-8-88615-308-8 (Ebook)

Inks and Bindings
888-290-5218
www.inksandbindings.com
orders@inksandbindings.com

CONTENTS

Languages of the World

Afrikaans
Arabic
Aramaic
Chinese
English
Flemish
French
Gaelic
German
Greek
Hebrew
Italian
Japanese
Latin
Portuguese
Russian
Sanskrit
Semitic
Spanish
Yiddish

Introduction

L et us change the world; Adam did, so can we. Everything God made was good, not only it was good, but it was also very good for the Lord himself said so. Until the disobedience of Adam. Therefore, if worse comes with disobedience, better will come with obedience. I can't promise that God will eliminate the days of judgment, but I can promise the right-hand side of God. When one lives on the side of obedience, red, yellow, black, and white covers all the nationalities of the world for they are all so precious in God's sight. Let us consider which is of the now and the result and that which of the could be and the result and then decide which is the most beneficial for man's life. For in righteousness of God, the thought pattern changes. Hate for another person or race no longer exist. And if anger does arrive, it is overpowered by the "Do unto others as you would have them to do unto you"; a God-given strength overpower that which is contrary. And love is the one medication for the heart, which would rid the world of everything that is destructive and causes confusion one for the other. The thought pattern will take on a new attitude which consist of these things.

"That ye might walk worthy of the Lord unto all pleasing being fruitful in every good work, and increasing in the knowledge of God" (Col. 1:10). For in the word of God is everything that is necessary to live the life God wants all people to live, all the dos and the don'ts which is inherited and which is avoided, and the result of them both is the same when Simon Peter said unto them, "I go a fishing." Therefore, let us go a fishing in the word of God, and when heed is taken, the result would be of a new lifestyle. This would make the world a better place. For in the whole word of God, we will come to the understanding of accepting the good and rejecting the evil and the result of them both.

As it is said that the mind is a terrible thing to waste, it is more horrific to lose one soul, the part of God that he give unto man, the part that which never dies. As the people that was on one accord to build a tower whose top may reach unto heaven, let us get on one accord to make this world a better place. It starts with two, then the two will start the change of the world; contrary to the domino effect in which you touch one and they all fall down, start with one and they all stand up. It's time to start an uprising not for rebellion but for building up. It takes more than climate change to make this world a better place to live in, but people change also in the parable of the sower; we all need to become a good ground for the word to fall on in order to produce the crop of godly living.

Not just mankind, nature itself will change for the better. The scripture says, "And God said unto Adam, 'Because thou hast harkened unto the voice of thy wife and hast eaten of the tree, of which I commanded saying thou shalt not eat of it; cursed is the ground for thy sake.'" Letting us know less sin, less destructive of nature for in the word of God, not just about to behavior of mankind but that of nature also. Therefore, when more of us is no longer a part of the problems, things will become better, and the result is a better world to live in. The control for climate change depends on mankind's change. I'm not saying that things will be the way it was before sin entered into the world, but a world with less sin will make the world which is now in existence. When Peter said, "I go fishing," it was food for the stomach, but this fishing, which is the word of God, is for the heart. And it lets us know what to keep and what to throw back and which to avoid and what should be kept and the result thereof.

Jesus is coming back for a church "people" that is without spot or wrinkle — that is, by the person of Jesus himself. He makes it possible therefore in following his example; the result is to become of God. If Adam, being one man, changed the world by disobeying God, let us consider what a multitude can do by being obedient. We cannot do this on our own ability but through Jesus Christ. He can show us a way of life that we know not of which is beyond the normal routine, and this comes about in knowing what God has in store for his people who are living according to his say so; therefore, let us get started.

"Forgetting One's Purpose"

They answered and said to Him, "Abraham is our father." Jesus said to them, "If you were Abraham's children, you would do the works of Abraham. But now you seek to kill Me, a man who has told you the truth which I heard from God. Abraham did not do this. You do the deeds of your father." Then they said to Him, "We were not born of fornication; we have one Father—God." Jesus said to them, "If God were your Father, you would love Me, for I proceeded forth and came from God; nor have I come of Myself, but He sent Me. Why do you not understand My speech? Because you are not able to listen to My word. You are of your father the devil, and the desires of your father you want to do. He was a murderer from the beginning, and does not stand in the truth, because there is no truth in him. When he speaks a lie, he speaks from his own resources, for he is a liar and the father of it." (John 8:39– 44 NMV)

Then Paul and Barnabas grew bold and said, "It was necessary that the word of God should be spoken to you first; but since you reject it, and judge yourselves unworthy of everlasting life, behold, we turn to the Gentiles. For so the Lord has commanded us: 'I have set you as a light to the Gentiles, That you should be for salvation to the ends of the earth.'" Now when the Gentiles heard this, they were glad and gloried the word of the Lord. And as many as had been appointed to eternal life believed. And the word of the Lord was being spread throughout all the region. But the Jews stirred up the devout and prominent women and the chief men of the city, raised up persecution against Paul and Barnabas, and expelled them from their region. (Acts 13:46–50 NKJV)

But the Jews stirred honorable women and the chief men of the city and raised persecution against Paul and Barnabas and expelled them out of their costs. Using the topic "Forgetting one's Purpose," a responsibility given, a person or thing is responsible for forgetting one's purpose by not doing what is assigned by the Lord. For the scripture tells us that in time past, God has allowed all nations to walk their own ways, but the time came that man no longer should live the rest of his time in the flesh to the desires of men but to the will of God. And he had to start somewhere; therefore, his call went out to a man named Abram, whom he changed his name to Abraham. When the Pharisees said unto Jesus "Abraham is our father" but being descendants of Abraham is not important, but being called by God for a purpose and Abraham being obedient is important, then Jesus let them know that the true children of Abraham would not seek to kill him but would join in the movement, representing who God is. They allowed dangerous words to come out of their mouth; perhaps, they didn't know it is a dangerous thing to fall into the hands of an angry God.

Not knowing the full scope of who Jesus was, him being conceived by the Holy Spirit, the Jews accused him of being born of fornication. With Mary not being married to Joseph at the time, the Jews said unto him, "We be not born of fornication. We have one father, even God," implying that God was their father. But the scripture let us to know, "'A son honoreth his father and a servant his master, if then I be a father where is my honor? And if I be a master where is my fear?' Saith the Lord of host unto you." It is said to the same people who said, "We want a God that we can see, here he is," and they see him not for Jesus who is the God that we can see, but they were implying that Mary was with child before she married Joseph. Be careful, little eyes, what you see, be careful, little mouth, what you say for it is not what goes into the mouth of man that devour him but what comes out, not the bread one eat but the words one say.

"Jesus said unto them, 'If God were your father, ye would love me for I proceeded forth and came from God, neither come I of myself, but he sent me'" (John 8:42). I have heard one said that God blinded their eyes from knowing who Jesus was because they would not kill him, but they blinded their own eyes. God don't give us a thing to know then turn around and keep you from knowing it for the blindness is in the fault of man, the ones that God called to be a light to other nations. For Jesus said, "Why do you understand my speech? Ye cannot hear my word if they who doing the will of God." They would know who Jesus was and understand his speech; it was not the intention of God for them not to know who Jesus was for many believed him for who he was for Simon Peter said unto him, "We believe and are sure that thou art the Christ, the son of the living God." But when one think more highly of themselves than they ought to, they should be a servant for God's purpose is to show the goodness in their lives so that others may see the good works of God in their lives and want to be partakers thereof. But Jesus let them know, "You are of your father the devil. And the lust of your father ye will do. And like father children, the devil come to steal, kill, and destroy." They wanted Jesus dead, and all who tried to hinder God's purpose is of the devil. And therefore to claim Abraham is their father, letting us know that one person cannot be in a right relationship with God because of another person's obedience to Him, we must work out our own salvation.

Acts 13:44–45 tells us, "And the next Sabbath day came almost the whole city together to hear the word of God. But when the Jews saw the multitudes, they were filled with envy, and spoke against those things which were spoken by Paul, contradicting and blaspheming." Perhaps, they didn't know when God decided to call man to the purpose of which they were created. Abraham, who came from the city of Ur and a gentile, became the first Hebrew to receive revelation from God. "And curse them that curse thee; and in thee shall all the families of the earth shall be blessed" (Gen. 12:3).

"For Paul said, 'What then? Are we better than they? No, in no wise; for we have before proved both Jews and Gentiles, that they are all under sin'" (Rom. 3:9). And when God told Abraham "I will make thee father of many nations," perhaps they didn't know that would include the rest of the nations of the world. The attitude of having God for myself and not for anyone else is not having God at all, forgetting that their purpose was to be an example before other nations, that they themselves would commit to the ordinance of the Lord. For God is enough for everybody for all sufficiency is in him as I have heard one said "He complete me."

Instead of welcoming the Gentile into the fold, they themselves showed the attitude of "if God is for you, then I am not for him." There is a saying "You have put your food in your mouth." It means that which come out of your mouth, you will regret it later. The scripture let us know if we suffer with him, we shall also reign with him; if we deny him, he also will deny us. Therefore, if I had wings like an eagle, I would fly all over this world, telling the good news of Jesus Christ. Not just by word only but also by experience, of what he did and still doing in my life. For if it wasn't for the good Lord on my side, I couldn't say amen, giving assent to everything that he said.

"Then Paul and Barnabas walked bold and said, 'It was necessary that the word of God should first have been spoken to you.'" They were doing as Jesus said, "Go ye first to the lost sheep of the house of Israel. And when there is a first, it means more is to be added." And if you don't except somebody will, God's word cannot be stopped no matter how much the opposition tries. For the scripture tells that the grass withered and the flower fadeth, but the word of God shall stand forever. Paul said, "For so hath the Lord commanded us saying, 'I have set thee to be a light of the Gentiles.'" Jesus said, "Aye are the light of the world a city that is set on a hill cannot be hid and when you let it shine before men that they may see your good works. And glorify your father which is in heaven."

When the Gentiles saw it in Paul and Barnabas, they were glad and glorified the word of the Lord, letting us know that there is still somebody out there that will hear the word of God and cry out "I yield, what must I do to be saved" for heaven is not full yet. All whom God hast called into his kingdom is not complete for if it were, Jesus would have already come to receive his church unto himself, letting me know that there is a work that I must do. He said, "Ye are the salt of the earth, but if the salt have lost his savor, wherewith shall it be salted?"

You are a preserver in a decaying world, but if the salt have lost his savor, where shall it be salted? It is, therefore, good for nothing but to be cast out and be trodden under the foot of men. When I was in pain, I asked the Lord if I could retire from ministry, but he didn't make me well to stand still. I got to tell somebody about Jesus; in him is a place where the righteous shall never be removed, the one that can remove sorrow from the heart and put away evil from the flesh. He is the one that said "If ye have faith as a grain of mustard seed, ye shall say unto this mountain, remove hence to yonder place; and it shall be remove and nothing shall be impossible unto you, the ones which is connected to Jesus Christ."

When the debit is greater than the increased, that which going out is greater than that which is coming in, when it costs more to live than what we have to live off, and everything is still all right, we owe it all to Jesus. King David said, "I was young and now I am old, I have never seen the righteous forsaken or his seed begging bread." There is so much to tell about Jesus for the scripture tells us, "And upon the first day of the week when the disciples come together to break bread, Paul preached unto them, ready to depart on the morrow; and continued his speech until midnight." One can preach long about Jesus and yet can't tell it all. And there are also many other things which Jesus did, that if they should be written by everyone, I suppose that even the world itself could not contain all the books, letting us know that there is much to tell about. Some things can be told and come to end, but not with Jesus. Acts 13:50 tells us, "But the Jews stirred up the devout and honorable women and the chief men of the city, and raised persecution against Paul and Barnabas, and expelled them out of their coasts."

If you don't accept it, someone else will for Paul was an ambassador for Christ, going from one country to another; even in bonds, he didn't allow that to prevent from speaking boldly as he ought to speak concerning Jesus Christ. He kept on doing what he was supposed to do. Some things in life is just for the purpose of one's self, but Jesus is not one of them for everybody ought to know who Jesus is. And trying to conceal him, he is not part of oneself. As Paul said, "For I am not ashamed of the gospel of Christ for it is the power of God unto salvation to everyone that believeth and the Jesus in me hath put the desire in me to tell however and whenever about who he is, therefore come let us adore him bow down before him and tell somebody who he is for he is Emmanuel."

"As Long as Breath Is in the Body, There Is Still a Chance with Jesus"

A cts 8:35–38 reads, "Then Philip opened His mouth and began at the same scripture, and preached unto him Jesus and they went on their way, they came unto a certain water. And the eunuch said, 'See here is water, what doth hinder me to be baptized.' And Philip said, 'If thou believeth with all thine heart thou mayest,' and he answered and said, 'I believe that Jesus Christ is the son of God.' And he commanded the Chariot to stand still and they went down both into the water, both Philip and the eunuch, and he baptized him."

"And one of the malefactors which was hung smiled on him saying, 'If thou be the Christ, save thyself and us,' but the other rebuked him seeing, 'Dost not thou fear God, saying thou art in the same condemnation, and we indeed justly, for we received the due reward of our deeds, but this man hath done nothing amiss.' And he said unto Jesus, 'Lord, remember me when thou comest into thy kingdom.' And Jesus said unto him, 'Verily I say unto thee, today shalt thou be with me in paradise'" (Luke 23:39–43).

There are many circumstances in life that can prevent mankind from achieving a desired purpose to young or old physical conditions and even gender, but being with

Jesus is not one of them for as long as breath is in the body, there is still a chance to be with Jesus. This message is not to encourage anyone to wait until the deathbed; seek the Lord while he may be found. "For no man know the hour nor the day that he will return, and that which came down from heaven was holy and that which goes back must be holy also." For Jesus came in the image of man, that man might become in the image of God. For he said that the Son of Man has come to seek and to save that which lost. An imperfect beginning to develop into that which is perfect. For he tells us, "Be ye therefore perfect even as your father which is in heaven is perfect." Jesus told a parable about a land owner and laborers who worked in his vineyard, an earthly saying with spiritual meanings.

The vineyard is the kingdom of God, the hour is the time that one put their hand to the gospel plow, and the wages is salvation. Salvation doesn't come in different amounts, one either have it or they don't; there is a saying that the early bird gets the worm. But in this case, the johnnies come late and get the worm also. As long as the door is not shut as it was with the five foolish virgins, for Jesus said, "Behold, I stand at the door and knock if any man hears my voice and open the door, I will come in to him and will sup with him, and he with me." And just as his mission on earth was of a limited time, so is his knocking in heaven for the day of judgment must come to pass for it tells us in the parable, "and when he had agreed with the workers for a penny a day, he sent them into vineyard." It lets us know that the work that we do for the Lord cannot be of our own choosing but that which he sends one to do as he said unto Peter, "Feed my lambs, feed my sheep."

On the outside of being sent comes a sounding brass or tinkling cymbal; the word doesn't fit in the word, it doesn't serve the purpose of which it is needed. Dying plants don't need sunshine but rain. And Jesus went out about the third hour and saw others standing idle in the marketplace. An idle mind is one that doesn't have a purpose, and God didn't make anyone to be fruitless. We might be rejected by man, but Jesus doesn't want any of us to be idle. And he said unto them, "Go ye also into the vineyard and whatsoever is right I will give you." And they went their way, letting us know that someone is taking heed to the invite. God is not slack concerning his promise but is long- suffering to us ward, not willing that any should perish but all should come to repentance. For any slackness is on the side of man, letting me know not to give up on Tom, Dick, and Harry no matter what lifestyle they might be living in now for there is still a chance with Jesus. I want to give warning every chance I got, to let it be known that the wages of sin is death, but the gift of God through Jesus Christ is eternal life. In order for one to receive it, they must confess with their mouth the Lord Jesus and shall believe in thine heart that God hath raised him from the dead. Thou shalt be saved, and the result is the different in one's lifestyle.

We can't say that we are of the Lord and still living in the sins of the world; therefore, the rest of my days, under the permission of the Lord, I'm going to tell his word as it is necessary. It is more to his word that God is good and his mercy refreshes evermore, but man must live by every word that proceed out of the mouth of the living God. I can't allow one to think that everything is all right when they are not living as an upright lifestyle. Try the spirit by the spirit and see whether it be of God or not. As Habakkuk said, "I will stand upon my watch and will watch to see what he will say unto me, and what I shall answer when I am reproved. And the Lord answered me and said, 'Write the vision, and make it plain upon tablet, that he may run that readeth it."

I will run out of sin into the arms of Jesus for he is still in the vineyard accepting all those that comes for time is drawing nigh for the sixth and the ninth hour. I passed and went, and the last is at hand. And it is up to him to do what he will with that which belongs unto him. "Has not the potter power over the clay, of the same lump, made one vessel unto honor?"

"And the angel of the Lord spoke unto Philip saying, 'Arise and go toward the south unto the way that goeth down from Jerusalem unto Gaza which is the desert'" (Acts 8:26). And there he found an Ethiopian reading Isaiah, the one with the lack of understanding. You see, everybody needs to know who Jesus is for there is not a day go by in my life that I don't want to know more about my Jesus to the point that I become as he is, void of everything that is contrary to a God who ordains live as Philip with the Ethiopian. Then Philip opened his mouth and began at the same scripture, the one that he was reading without understanding, and he preached unto him Jesus. And he wanted to be baptized an outward appearance of an inward profession.

The belief in the heart that Jesus Christ is the son of God and the result is holy living for God said, "Be ye holy for I am holy for you see when one comes to the Lord, it is rejoicing time." Philip went on his way rejoicing. The thief on the cross didn't take an opportunity to learn of who Jesus was as Nicodemus did, the one that came to Jesus by night; he realized that what he did know is not all that he should know. As Paul said unto Timothy, "Study to show thyself approve, rightly dividing the word of truth." Jesus let him know you must be born again for flesh and blood cannot enter into the kingdom of God, but one must be born of the spirit.

And the thief was not like the Ethiopian ready to understand the meaning of the word of God for he was a thief and his life consisted of taking that which didn't belong to him, but while hanging on the cross, he was on the right-hand side of Jesus. You see, it is good to be on the right-hand side of Jesus. Unlike the mother of Zebedee's children who went to Jesus requesting that when he goes into his kingdom, one of her sons should be on his right and the other should be on his left, desiring what seems to them to be of high positions. But like David said, "I rather be a door keeper in the house of God than to dwell in a wide space where there is wickedness."

Some see being a minister as a high position, but they came down from there for the way up is down. One should not think more highly of themselves than they ought to for Jesus said, but he that is greater among you shall be your servant, whosoever shall exalt himself shall be abased, and he that humble himself shall be exalted.

You see, outward appearance doesn't always speak for that which is lurking on the inside for Luke tells us that and one of the malefactors which were hanged railed on him, using abusive words and saying, "If you are who you say you are, which is the Christ, save thyself and us." What he didn't know was that if Jesus had gotten down off the cross, his chance for salvation would be of nonexistent not only for himself but also for whosoever else. But the thief on the other side rebuked him saying, "Dost not thou fear God, seeing thou art in the same condemnation?" The appearance was the same but not the facts; they were there because of what they did. But Jesus was there not because of any wrong he did, but because to right the wrong that we all did for all have come short of the glory of God. And no self-doing can make those amend. He let him know we are getting what we justly deserve, but this man has done nothing wrong. His eye was opened to fact of who Jesus was as some of us. One day our eyes are open to the fact of who Jesus is, and we believed and received his gift of eternal life. And he said unto Jesus, "Lord, remember me when thou comes into thy kingdom." You see, it is good to be on the right-hand side of Jesus while life is still in the mortal body for in it is still a chance to be with him. He didn't have that chance as it was with Zacchaeus, the day that Jesus was at his house, for he stood and said unto the Lord, "Behold Lord the half of my goods I give to the poor; and if I have taken anything from any man by false accusations, I restore him fourfold."

He realized that he couldn't do the wrong things and still be in the righteous of God. "Jesus said unto him, 'This day is salvation came to this house, for so much as he also is a son of Abraham'" (Luke19:9). He no longer conformed but has been transformed by the renewing of his mind for this is what Jesus came to do to seek and save that which was lost; there is still a chance with Jesus. The thief that said unto Jesus, "Lord remember me when thou cometh into thy kingdom," didn't had the chance to make amends for that which he had received unjustly or to be water baptized as it was with the Ethiopians, but Jesus said unto him, "Verily I say unto thee, today shall thou be with me in paradise." He knew he was going to die, the chance to be converted was available to him, but death can come unaware as it was with Nabal, the one that refused to give help to God's people for the scripture tells us, "But it came to pass in the morning, when the wine was gone out of Nabal and these things, there these things is the good that she (his wife) had did, which he wouldn't do, his heart couldn't take it, and it died within him, and became as a stone." It lets me know the blood is still running warm in my vein. And if the righteous scarcely be saved, where shall the ungodly and sinners appear? If every one that was to be saved is already saved, he would have already come back, but there are others that are coming into the fold and need to know the whole Word of God before going into the promised land.

Moses did not only give the people God's word of blessings if they do good but also warnings if they do evil. In the good news of Jesus, it's not only which should be kept, but also which should be done away with. As Paul said unto the Corinthians, "In the name of our Lord Jesus Christ, when ye are gathered together and my spirit, with the power of our Lord Jesus Christ, to deliver my such an one unto Satan for the destruction of the flesh, that the spirit may be saved in the day of the Lord Jesus, your glorying is not good, know ye not that a little leaven leaveneth whole lump."

God said unto Jeremiah, "What do you see, Jeremiah?" And he said, "Two baskets of figs, one had very good figs and the naughty figs, but with right words, hast a chance to enter into the basket of the good figs." If everyone was right with the Lord, he would have already come back, but there are others that are coming into the fold and need to know the necessary steps that must be taken and what to void. They don't want to be a stumbling block in the way of preventing someone else from coming unto the offer or receive the offer of salvation but letting them know the whole word of God, his approval, as well as his disapproval.

I have heard one said, "If you are going to sin, all you have to do is to ask God to forgive you." But live according to the whole word of God, and sin will no longer reign in one members for when one is working in the vineyard of Jesus every hour of day, one is fixed for eternal life. I have heard people say from a financial stand point I am fix for life, which is physical life, but in the vineyard of Jesus, we are fixed for eternal life.

Messing Up a Good Thing

And he tarried seven days, according to the set time that Samuel had appointed: but Samuel came not to Gilgal; and the people were scattered from him. And Saul said, "Bring hither a burnt offering to me, and peace offerings." And he offered the burnt offering. And it came to pass, that as soon as he had made an end of offering the burnt offering, behold, Samuel came; and Saul went out to meet him, that he might salute him. And Samuel said, "What hast thou done?" And Saul said, "Because I saw that the people were scattered from me, and that thou camest not within the days appointed, and that the Philistines gathered themselves together at Michmash; Therefore, said I, The Philistines will come down now upon me to Gilgal, and I have not made supplication unto the Lord: I forced myself therefore, and offered a burnt offering." And Samuel said to Saul, "Thou hast done foolishly: thou hast not kept the commandment of the Lord thy God, which he commanded thee: for now would the Lord have established thy kingdom upon Israel forever. But now thy kingdom shall not continue: The Lord have sought him a man after his own heart, and the Lord hath commanded him to be captain over his people, because thou hast not kept that which the Lord commanded thee. For now, would the Lord have established thy kingdom of Israel forever, but now thy kingdom shall not continue; the Lord hath sought him. A man after his own heart, and the lord hath commanded him to be a captain over his people, because thou hast not kept that which the Lord commanded thee." (1 Sam. 13:8–14)

And five of them were wise, and five were foolish. They that were foolish took their lamps, and took no oil with them. (Matt. 25:2–3)

For if we sin willfully after that we have received the knowledge of the truth, there remaineth no more sacrifice for sins, but a certain fearful look of judgment and fiery indignation, which shall devour the adversaries. (Heb. 10:26– 27)

Taking on a role of that which should not be, to interfere with, to come between, or to prevent, modifies the result or course of events. When Moses and the children of Israel was in a tricks and between situation — the Red Sea before them and pharaoh's army closing in behind — he didn't take the role of a priest but waited for the voice of the Lord which said, "Stretch out thine hand over the sea," and the result was that which intended from the Lord. One can't do anything for God which is not assigned to one hand, messing up a good thing did not start with King Saul but the first man and the first woman that God handmade and placed in the garden of Eden. He told them how they should live and that death was nowhere in the picture. Not only did they bought it upon themselves, but also to everybody else as I heard it have been said to open a can of worms. The Samuel scripture saith that Samuel came not to Gilgad; just because Samuel was there didn't mean that God wasn't. As the song said, "If there's a problem you can't handle, look up."

Be of good courage and wait upon the Lord, and he shall direct your heart, and because the people were scattered from him doesn't mean that God saw fit to make him king. With that came the promise of his protection of keeping as long as he stayed under the guidelines of a king.

"And Saul said, 'Bring hither a burnt offering to me and peace offerings,'" but when one is operating on the outside of the will of God, there is no peace. We see it in the world every day; instead of asking the Lord for help in the static of a king, he took on the role of a priest and did that which is contrary to the will of God. The scripture said to "wait on the Lord and keep his way and he shall exalt thee to inherit land; when the wicked are cut off, thou shalt see it." And again David said, "I have seen the wicked in great power, and spreading himself like a green bay tree, yet he passed away, no matter how big the multitude of the Philistines was."

God is greater. Being one with God is more than the whole world against you; you don't need to worry about the wrong people in office.

Greater is the God of heaven. And it came to pass that as soon as he had made an end of burnt offerings, behold Samuel came, and Saul went out to meet him that he might salute him. But instead of a salute from Samuel came a denouncement. "What hast thou done?" Saul tried to put the blame on someone else as Adam did. "The woman whom thou gavest to be with me, she gave me of the tree and I did eat, but the scripture let us to know. He that covereth his sin shall not prosper; but whose confesseth and forsaketh them shall have mercy."

One is of no benefit without the other. Saul tried to justify himself, "I saw the people were scattered from me and you were not here." When desperation set in, in all your ways acknowledge him, and he shall direct your path for the outcome is not of Samuel but of God. Saul as he saw it, desperate means calls for desperate measures, so he found himself therefore and offered a burnt offering; in other words, it wasn't what he wanted to do but what he had to do as he saw it, letting us know that one can't do for God which is not assign to one's hand. He allowed fear to override the trust that is in the Lord when the scriptures let us to know that it is better to trust in the Lord than to put confidence in man; he had more confidence in the Philistines than in the Lord that made him king.

And instead of and add to it, it was a take away from. "For Samuel said to Saul, 'Thou hast done foolishly.'" Samuel, a true servant of the Lord, didn't go along to get along; as the saying goes, "sweep it under the rug." Open rebuke is better than secret love, better to speak the truth to a strayed person than to let it slide. A right way and right speaking must match. Anything else is a partaker thereof. Samuel let Saul know, "Thou hast not kept the commandment of the Lord thy God, which he commanded thee." Then he gave him the result of how things would have been if he had stayed in the pathway of righteousness; not only did he mess up for himself, but also for others who would have been no more kings from the tribe of the Benjamite, no more of the line that the savior of the world would come through. Samuel let him know that future kings will not come through the line of Saul. Samuel let him know for now that the Lord have established the kingdom upon Israel forever. But God knew that. Saul was going to mess up even before the set up.

Genesis tells us concerning Judah, "The scripture shall not depart from Judah, not a lawgiver from between his feet, until Shiloh came; and unto him hall the gathering of the people be, no longer through the line of the Benjamites." Samuel let Saul know that his kingdom shall not continue because of his sins, letting me know that which isn't should not be treated like that, which is for in doing right also consist of standing against which is wrong. Paul's words to Timothy was, "Them that sin rebuke before all, that others also may fear, a saying of the world is called a spade." Samuel let Saul know that "the Lord hath sought him a man after his own heart, and the Lord hath commanded him to be captain over his people." With the command came the ability, and the result should be to take heed and not to try to modify or prevent the result or course of events. If we could do that to ourselves, there would not be a need for a God for what does man have that he didn't receive from God? As the Psalm said, "I will sing unto the Lord so long as I live; I will sing praise to my God while I have my being."

A life of commitment to the Lord, and it also let us know that if one don't do God's will according to his standard, he is not going to keep one on. The Lord has sought him a man after his own heart, a demonstration of how one must live and or what character one must process to be a servant of the Most High God. It lets me know that just anything will not do for if he is called on, on the outside of a godly heart, he will not show up. As in the showdown on Mount Carmel, the prophet of Baal call on Baal, and he did not show up, letting us know if we want God to show up on our behalf, we must do what he said for which one sees as a help, when it comes to the will of God, who can hinder him for he does God all by himself. And all the help that is needed is from the side of man. He is the one who aid, assist, and provide the necessary strength that is needed to perform which he assigned to one's hand. David said, "Hide not thy face from me; put not thy servant away in anger, thou hast been my help; leave me not, neither forsake, O God, of my salvation." Then it said, "God is our refuge and strength, a very present help in time of trouble."

As Proverbs said concerning the parents, "Train up a child in the way he shall go; and when he is old, he will not depart from it." When God train up a Christian, they better not depart from him for the chance of return may not be available because the door might be shut as it was with the five foolish virgins; there is no mind that so complicated and defused that God can't transform. Let us take a look at Mary Magdalene who had been possessed with seven demons. But this was before she met Jesus. Jesus was having dinner at Simon the Pharisee's house. And behold, a woman in the city, who was a sinner, knew that Jesus ate meat she brought an alabaster box of ointment, stood at his feet behind him weeping. Weeping may endure for a night, but joy comes in the morning. She began to wash his feet with tears, wipe them with the hair of her head, kissed his feet, and anointed them with the ointment. But when his disciples saw it, they had indignation, saying, "To what purpose is this waste?" This ointment might have been sold for much, what they saw as a waste was an act of grace. For all the money in the world cannot save one soul from destruction. Jesus said, "No man came to me except the Father which hath sent me draw him, and what God that put together let no man put asunder."

When Jesus said "Why trouble ye the woman?" it wasn't just for the disciples only but all that which was against her. She was no longer demon possessed but a new creation in Christ Jesus; she was no longer who she once was. She became dedicated to the purpose of Jesus. She was there when his disciples wasn't when they nailed him to the cross. Mary was there. She was the first person who saw him after his resurrection, the one that Jesus said unto the woman, "Why weepeth thou?" She was supposing him to be the gardener and said unto him, "Sir, if thou have moved him form here, tell me where you have put him and I'll go and get him."

Jesus had told Simon about the creditor and the two debtors. One owed more than the other but neither could pay. He asked which of them would love him most. Simon answered, "I suppose that he to whom he forgave most."

Mary loved her Jesus, but I love my Jesus. Jesus said unto her, "Mary." Then she knew this was Jesus for the sheep of Jesus knows his voice. She got excited, turn herself, and said unto him, "Rabbi." It means master, which he rightly is for he can do which no one else can do; he can take away which should not be and replace it with which should be, and there is no limitation in his acts of love for the things he does for one, he will do for all. As the song said, "What you need, God got it, he got everything that you need."

There is nothing broken that God can't fix. In the parable of the ten virgins, it lets us know that God is a fair God; he doesn't discriminate against anyone. He is a God of equal opportunity. Five of the virgins was wise and five was foolish, but they all had a choice to meet the bridegroom. The five wise took their hands of their lives and gave God control, and the five foolish was of the verbal and not in possession; they talked the talk but not the walk, profession without procession, messing up a good thing. The scripture said, "Whomsoever will, let them come." Why settle for pretending when the real is there for the asking? The five wise represents the true church of God while the five foolish are just pretenders, professors and not possessors. The scripture lets us to know, "God will destroy them that speak falsehood."

I didn't tell anybody I know the Lord before I knew the Lord, but since I am of God, I got to tell it much; way maker and promise-keeper, you can take him at his word.

Being of the Right Comeback

Verily, verily, I say unto you, the hour is coming, and now is, when the dead shall hear the voice of the Son of God: and they that hear shall live. For as the Father hath life in himself; so hath he given to the Son to have life in himself; And hath given him authority to execute judgment also, because he is the Son of man. Marvel not at this: for the hour is coming, in the which all that are in the graves shall hear his voice, And shall come forth; they that have done good, unto the resurrection of life; and they that have done evil, unto the resurrection of damnation. I can of mine own self do nothing: as I hear, I judge: and my judgment is just; because I seek not mine own will, but the will of the Father which hath sent me. If I bear witness of myself, my witness is not true. (John 5:25–31)

For ye were as sheep going astray; but are now returned unto the Shepherd and Bishop of your souls. For you were straying like sheep, but have now returned to the Shepherd and Overseer of your souls. (1 Pet. 2:25)

Using for a subject "Being of the Right Comeback" is to be converted to another person's opinion, to be brought to a specified situation of being in one state to another, from the way down to the way up. Moses's last address to Israel was about how they should live when they get into the promised land if they did the will of God. They had his protection, and if they did which is contrary, the wrath of God would come upon them. But this message is not about how to act when one gets to heaven, but it is how to act in order to get to heaven or one is not going there. You see, heaven is not like Canaan wherein you do the will of God when you get there, but with heaven, the will of God must be done in order to get there. It was flesh and blood that went into the land of Canaan which is of the natural, and they had to fight in order to take possession of the land. But in heaven, the battle is over, no more wrestling between principalities, against powers, against the ruler of the darkness of this world for heaven is a prepared place for prepared people, which began with confession with the mouth and believing in the heart that God had raised Jesus from the dead. Thou shall be saved. Somebody is claiming something that they don't have in this the same old world, which will be of non-existence. The scriptures let us to know that one cannot serve God and mammon; there is no such thing as an in-between life. As some said, straddle the fence for in Jesus, all intended sin becomes nonexistent as we live and grow in the knowledge of our Lord and Savior Jesus Christ, and the result is of the growing in grace. For God doesn't have a halfway house as the prison system do, it's not bad enough to be in a cell but not good enough to be set completely free.

We can use the Apostle Paul as a perfect example, one that went from darkness to light for he was not ashamed of the gospel of Christ; it is the power of God unto salvation to everyone who believed, to the Jews first and also to the Greek. For therein is the righteousness of God revealed from faith to faith; as it is written, the just shall live by faith which is not seen with the nature's eyes but seen with the heart, being of the right comeback.

There are many comebacks that can take place in a person life. But the most important of them all is to be converted to another person's opinion, and that person is Jesus Christ. Saul the persecutor became Paul who became Paul the believer. He was the one who said to live is Christ and to die is gain, to be absent from the body is to be present with the Lord. "Follow me as I follow Christ." There are some things in life we don't know the end until it come upon us. There's a song that said, "I'm going to run on and see what the end will be." But the scriptures let us to know what the end is going to be before it is the end. Lord, who shall abide in your tabernacle? Who shall dwell in your holy hill? He that walketh uprightly and worketh righteousness and speaketh the truth in his heart, no one left in limbo, waiting for a decision to be made. As Joshua said unto the people of Israel, "And if it seem evil unto you to serve the Lord, choose you this day whom ye will serve."

There is a place for those that do and there's a place for those that don't for God's word is in detail from start to finish. Jesus tells us, "Verily, verily I say unto you, the hour is coming, and now is when the dead shall hear the voice of the son of God; and they that hear shall live not talking about you and me, but those who had pass on before there was one more sacrifice for sin they will have a chance to be redeem."

The scripture tells you in Ephesians 5:14, "Wherefore he saith, awake thou that sleepest, and arise from the dead, and Christ shall give thee light." There is a saying, when you are dead, you are done, but Jesus is letting us know that physical death is not the end; there will be a coming back for the purpose of judgment and who shall be able to stand. As the Father has life in himself, so he has given to the Son to have life in himself. Life comes from God himself, so he have allowed the son to give life. If one wants to live, look to Jesus, letting us know you can't pass by Jesus and go to God. The Bible is the written word; Jesus is the speaking word, the word that became flesh. The one that the Father has given authority to execute judgment because he is the Son of Man.

Adam and Eve was handmade by the hands of God. In all other cases, one don't exist until they are born, but Jesus existed before he was flesh born. Daniel said, "I saw in the night visions and behold, one like the Son of Man come with the clouds of heaven, and came to the ancient of days, and they brought him near before him, and there was given him dominion and glory, and a kingdom that all people, nations, and languages should serve him." His dominion is an everlasting dominion, which shall not pass away, and his kingdom shall not be destroyed; who wouldn't want to be a part of a set up like that?

I have heard one said, "I am in love with Jesus." Love begets love, and that covers a multitude of sin, and having a measure of preventing the things I used to do, I don't do them anymore, living according to the rudiment of the world but of the standards that is ordained in a lifestyle that comes only through Jesus our Christ. Peter said, "He commanded us to preach unto the people, and to testify that it I he which was ordained of God to be the judge of quick and dead." And Jesus said, "Marvel not at this; for the hour is coming in which all that are in the graves shall hear his voice, and shall come forth; they that have done good, unto the resurrection of life; and that have done evil, unto the resurrection of damnation." It lets us know to make our election sure that it be of God and not of the contrary and whom to keep company with. The ones that don't live according to the judgment of God, for God do nots will always be do not. In the parable of Lazarus and the rich man, the rich man tried to change God's agenda, but God's word is an unchangeable menu; it is not like one of from a restaurant where you can swap one thing for another. We must live by every word that proceed out of the mouth of God; try the spirit by the spirit, and see whether it is of God or not.

Jesus said, "And they shall come forth, they that have done good, unto the resurrection of life and they that have done evil, unto the resurrection of damnation." It's the result of how we live in the bodies of that which we now have. Whether they are of God or not, the separation of the sheep from the goats, the wheat from the tare, the result of whom one chooses to serve again, I say that in some things, we don't know the end until it is upon us. The word of God lets us know the end before it approaches, giving us time for preparation, knowing that the ungodly shall not stand in the judgment or the sinners in the congregation of the righteous for the Lord knows the way of righteous and those of God should also know. He said, "Be not unequally yoked together with unbelievers; for what fellowship hath righteousness with unrighteousness; it is not what comes out to the mouth but what's in the heart, and what communion hath light with darkness; for the way of the ungodly shall perish." Jesus said, "I can of mine own self do nothing; as I hear, I judge and my judgment is just; because I seek not mine own will, but the will of the father which hath sent me."

Jesus, being in the form of God, thought it's not robbery to be equal with God but made himself of no reputation and took upon him the form of a servant and who made in the likeness of men. And being found in fashion as a man, he humbled himself and became obedient unto death, even the death on the cross. Perfect Jesus was obedient to the

Father and did according to what the Father said. David said, "Behold I was shapen in iniquity, and in sin did my mother conceive me."

As Jesus said unto Martha, "For she was burdened about much serving, thou not care that my sister left me to serve alone? Bid therefore that she helps me." Jesus answered and said unto her, "Martha, Martha, thou art careful and troubled about many things but one thing is needful; and Mary hath chosen that good part which shall not be taken away from her." It lets me know to let nothing get in the way of my concentrating on Jesus Christ; for you see, giving up sin is not the whole picture but an alliance must be formed. As the song said, "Have a little talk with Jesus, it will make everything aright."

Every so often, Jesus left the crowd and went up into the mountain to have a little talk with the Father. He said, "If I bear witness of myself, my witness is not true." It lets me know before I can tell it to you that I must first get it from Jesus. As Jesus said unto the church of the Laodicea, "I know thy works." As the saying goes, one might can fool man some of the time but can't fool God none of the time. One must be of the right comeback. "For ye were as sheep going astray; but are now natured unto the shepherd and bishop of your souls. For God lay in Zion a chief cornerstone elect, precious; and he that believeth shall not be confounded." And that stone is Jesus Christ, the one who said, "If I be lifted up from the earth, I will draw all men unto me." He was not talking about the cross but the ascension for he said to Mary, "Touch me not; for I am not yet ascended to my Father." He said to doubting Thomas, "Reach hither thy finger and behold my hands; and reach hither thy hand and thrust into my side; and be not faithless but believing, even ate fish with the disciples for no flesh and blood can inter into the kingdom of God." Some of his disciples had already witness the transfiguration for he is no longer the man Jesus but the Lord Jesus as he said unto Peter and Andrew his brother, "Follow me, and I will make you fishers of men." He is still making man children of God.

Doing What Jesus Said

And the Lord spoke unto Moses, saying, "Speak unto the children of Israel, and say unto them, Concerning the feasts of the Lord, which ye shall proclaim to be holy convocations, even these are my feasts. Six days shall work be done: but the seventh day is the sabbath of rest, an holy convocation; ye shall do no work therein: it is the sabbath of the Lord in all your dwellings." (Lev. 23:1)

After this there was a feast of the Jews; and Jesus went up to Jerusalem. Now there is at Jerusalem by the sheep market a pool, which is called in the Hebrew tongue Bethesda, having five porches. In these lay a great multitude of impotent folk, of blind, halt, withered, waiting for the moving of the water. For an angel went down at a certain season into the pool, and troubled the water: whosoever then first after the troubling of the water stepped in was made whole of whatsoever disease he had. And a certain man was there, which had an infirmity thirty and eight years. When Jesus saw him lie, and knew that he had been now a long time in that case, he saith unto him, "Wilt thou be made whole?" The impotent man answered him, "Sir, I have no man, when the water is troubled, to put me into the pool: but while I am coming, another steppeth down before me." Jesus saith unto him, "Rise, take up thy bed, and walk." And immediately the man was made whole, and took up his bed, and walked: and on the same day was the sabbath. (John 5:1–9)

J ust as at the wedding at Cana when they wanted wine and there was none, Jesus's mother said unto him that they have no wine. She said also unto the servants, "Whatever he saith unto you, do it." Jesus said unto them, "Fill the water pots with water." And they filled them up to the brim. The result was the best wine which Jesus caused to be doing. What Jesus said is best life that one can obtain. The Lord spoke to Moses, saying, "Speak unto the children of Israel and say unto them concerning the feast of the Lord which ye shall proclaim to be holy convocation, even these are my feast, the purpose is of showing honor to the Lord for what he had done in their lives brought them out of bondage and put a seal on them as being his people." And when it comes to verse three, it says, "This is what man is to do but not do, six days shall work he done but the seventh day is the Sabbath of rest." God knows the ability of man; they don't have mechanical power that they can go on and on without rest, and in that day of rest, there's a holy convocation, a coming together to give thanks unto the Lord. As David said, "I was glad when they said unto me let us go into the house of the Lord. Our feet shall stand within thy gate, O Jerusalem."

You see, the Sabbath is for the purpose of man and not of God for if God was to take a day off, things would not be as they are today for everything moves by the power of God. Our minds cannot apprehend what it would be like if God was to take a day off. I'm so glad that the scripture lets us know that at all times I will lift mine eyes unto the hills from where comes my help. "My help cometh from the Lord which made heaven and earth. He will not suffer thy foot to be moved he that keepeth thee will not slumber, behold, he that keepeth Israel shall neither slumber nor sleep." He is always on the move for the purpose of mankind; he was there at the pool of Bethesda while the feast of the Jews was going on, doing which God told them to do. Jesus is the Son of God, God in the flesh, doing which he came to do for he said, "I must work the works of him that sent me, while it is day: no specification of day that it shouldn't be done for the Sabbath is a day set aside for man rest and a time for approaching God with thanksgiving for his redemption acts which he has done in our lives." And if it wasn't for Jesus, there wouldn't be a Sabbath for he said unto them, "The Son of Man is Lord also of the Sabbath." It lets us know that he knew what the Sabbath is all about, and it is not about man telling God what to do but God telling man what to do, doing what Jesus said.

The scripture tells us, "Now there is at Jerusalem by the sheep market a pool, which I called in the Hebrew tongue Bethesda having five porches in these days a great multitude of impotent folks, what is sometime called people with handicap can't do for themselves because a hinder stands in the way." But as Paul said, "I can do all things through Jesus Christ which strengthen me." The man had been in this condition for thirty long years, not able to get to the pool on his own ability when the angel troubled the water. The abled bodies had an me first attitude and wouldn't help him into the pool, but Jesus let us to know that the first shall be last and the last shall be first. When Jesus saw him lie and know that he had been now a long time in that case, he said unto him, "Wilt thou be made whole." The scripture lets to know that there is no creature that is not manifested in his sight but all things are naked and opened unto the eyes of him with whom we have to do. Instead of saying make me whole, he stated the reason for him still being in his condition on someone else. The impotent man answered him, "See I have no man, when the water is troubled to put me in the pool, but while I am coming, another steppeth down before me." He didn't know who it was that said unto him "Wilt thou be made whole," neither did the woman at the well when she said unto him "Sir, give me this water, that I thirst not neither come hither to draw."

There is something in life that doesn't need hindsight to accept. Jesus said unto him, "Rise take up thy bed and walk and immediately." The man was made whole and took up his bed and walked. Isaiah said then, "The eyes of the blind opened, And the ears of the deaf shall be unstopped. Then shall the lame man leap as an hart, and the tongue of the dumb sing." It doesn't state any forbidden day. There is a saying, "Where does the elephant sit? The answer is anywhere he want to." God does whatever and whenever he wants to, and, therefore, I am going to do what Jesus said. If he said jump, I won't ask not why but how high for he said, "I am the vine ye are the branches, He that abideth in me and I in him, the same bringeth forth much fruit for without me you can do nothing and when you do this thing, it brings forth life and life more abundantly." And he did what Jesus said, and it was restored whole like the others.

In the case of the man with the dropsy, his body was retaining fluid, and he didn't have to go to the doctor to obtain fluid pills for Jesus took him and heal him and let him go. What a mighty God we serve. Angels bow before him, heaven and earth adore him. not only that Lazarus had been dead for four long days, but also in that length of time, the body has deteriorated for Martha said unto him, "He hast been dead four days by this time he stinketh." It lets us know that every stinketh situation, we might find ourselves in Jesus; he can bring us out of them like he said to the woman that was caught in the act of adultery, "Go and sin no more." Jesus said unto Lazarus, "Come forth." He that which was dead came forth.

Have any of you ever been in a situation where the only help was available in is of Jesus Christ? I have. Out of all that I been through down through the years, I didn't know there were pain to that magnitude existed. Being paralyzed by pain, I could barely call my daughter, Sharon, but we live in a long house, she on one end and I on the other. I said that I was going to be found dead in this bed in the morning, but I started talking to the Lord. In growing up, Robert was called little brother and I was called little sister. I said, "Lord, you have taken little brother, are you going to take little sister too? If so, I can't do a thing about it." I went to sleep talking to the Lord, but when morning came, I was able to get out of bed but still in pain. But as the scripture tells us that "weeping may endure for a night, but my morning hast come," and I am not in pain like that anymore. From the thought of death, the saying goes back in the saddle again. Back in sweet communion with Jesus Christ who wouldn't serve a God like that for on the outside of him is eternal damnation, but on the inside is eternal life. And this comes about in doing what he said. The blind would never have seen unless they did what Jesus said. The lame would never have walk unless they did what Jesus said. Salvation will never come in the heart unless we do what Jesus said for he said, "Come unto me, all ye that labors and are heavy laden and I will give you rest. You don't have to go through this on your own for I am here for you, take my yoke upon you and learn of me; for I am meek and lowly in heart; and ye shall find rest unto your soul." A yoke is a crossbar that hook two together, and when one is hooked to Jesus, oh, what a difference life is like. "For my yoke is easy and my burden is light." That heavy load of life comes into nonexistence.

As the song said, "I got rid of my heavy load," this came by doing what Jesus said. And he doesn't ask one to do a thing without giving the ability thereof for he said, Enter ye in at the strait gate; and if one don't, wide is the gate and broad is the way, that leadeth to destruction, and many there be which go in through it." You see, being yoke to Jesus is being combined, committed, and joined together for the same purpose. A part for Jesus to do and a part for us. A merger hast been made; it's not about all he do for us but what we do for him for he said, "Let your light so shine before man that they may see your good works and glorify your father which is in heaven."

When Samantha, at a very young age, spoke words that was beyond her age, one said she talked big girl talk. One day, we were parked in McDonald's parking lot. She saw a toy in the window and started saying, "I want that toy." Jimmy went running in McDonald's and came back with a Happy Meal with the toy inside that he forgot to get a straw, so he went running back in McDonald's and came back with a straw. Samantha said unto him, "I can count on you, Jimmy, and you can count on me." In this random life, it is not all about "I can count on you, Jesus" but "Jesus, you can count on me."

Jesus found Philip and said unto him, "Follow me." Philip found Nathan and said unto him, "We have found him of whom Moses in the law and the prophet did write, Jesus of Nazareth, the son of Joseph." Everybody ought to know who Jesus is for when one know who he is for themselves, they tell it to someone else. When the woman at the well found out who he was, she left her water pot at the well and went into the city and said, "Come see a man which told me all thing that I ever did." And when the man that Jesus told to take up thy bed and walk found out who Jesus was told the Jews that it was Jesus who make him whole. Jesus said, "For all the prophet and the law prophesied until John," but in Jesus, it's direct contact for he is God in the flesh. No more telling Moses to "tell pharaoh let my people go, no more talking"; no one told Isaiah to "tell my people come let us reason together"; no more sending Jonah to Nineveh that great city and cry against it. "For this wickedness is come up before me for Jesus said 'Behold, I stand at the door and knock, if any man hear my voice, and open the door, I will come into him, and will sup with him and he with me.'"

Keeping the Appointment of the Appointed Time

And there were certain men who were defiled by the dead body of a man: that they could not keep the Passover on that day; And they came before Moses and before Aaron on that day and those men said unto him, "We are defiled by the dead body of a man wherefore are we kept back, that we may not offer an offering of the Lord in his appointed season among the children of Israel." And Moses said unto them, "Stand still, and I will hear what the Lord will command concerning you. And the Lord will command concerning you." And the Lord spoke unto Moses saying, "Speak unto the children. If any man of you as of your posterity shall be unclean by reason of a dead body, or be in a journey afar off, yet he shall keep the Passover unto the Lord. The fourteenth day of the second month at even they shall keep it, and eat it with unleavened bread and bitter herbs. They shall leave none of it unto the morning, nor break any bone of it: according to the ordinances of the Passover they shall keep it. But the man that is clean, and is not in a journey, and forbeareth to keep the Passover, even the same soul shall be cut off from among his people: because he brought not the offering of the Lord in his appointed season, that man shall bear his sin. And if a stranger shall sojourn among you, and will keep the Passover unto the Lord; according to the ordinance of the Passover, and according to the manner thereof, so shall he do: ye shall have one ordinance, both for the stranger, and for him that was born in the land." (Num. 9:6–14)

"Appointed time" is an agreement to meet at a specific time at a specific place for a specific purpose. the Lord spoke unto Moses in the wildness of Sinai in the month of the second year after they came out of the land of Egypt, saying, "Let the children of Israel keep the Passover at his appointed season." A feast of the Jews which commemorates of the times when God smiting the firstborn of the Egyptians, Passover is the habitation of the Hebrews. The sixth verse tells us that there were certain men who were defiled by the dead body of a man. When the scripture said that "whosoever is defiled by the dead, both make male and female shall be put out, without the camp shall ye put them these defiled men came before Moses and Aaron on that day, and these men said unto him, 'We are defiled by the dead body of a man wherefore are we kept back.'"

I can understand these men for I, too, don't want to be kept back from the things of God, that's why I will do all things of God. They wanted to offer offering of the Lord in this appointed season among the children of Israel. And Moses said unto them, "Stand still, and I will hear what the Lord will command concerning you, if there is something one don't know and living according to the will of God for Jesus, let us to know. Ask and it shall be given you; seek and ye shall find, knock, and it shall be opened unto you, for God is a God of restitution. He can restore that which was taken away." When there seems to be no way, God can make a way for he said unto Moses, "Speak to the children of Israel, saying if any man of you or of your children shall be unclean by reason of a dead body, or be in a journey afar off, yet he shall keep the Passover unto the Lord." Two reasons God allowed for not taking part therein, but he is a God of restoration. He can restore which was taken away by proper means for he said, "Yet he shall keep the Passover unto the Lord." Here we see that validation comes into display. When there seems to be no way, God can make a way when Jesus said to the man, "Follow me." The man said, "First let me bury my father," but Jesus said unto the man, "Let the dead bury the dead."

Another benefit is when one stays in the thing which is related to the Lord, it blocks out which is contrary for it has a twofold purpose. "The fourteenth day of the second month at even they shall keep it, and eat with unleavened bread and bitter herbs." It lets us know that God is a God of a second chance; they let their request made known unto the Lord, and he received them with gladness. It is the result of wanting to keep the appointments of God for Jesus said, "Blessed are they that hear the word of God and keep it." And again he said, "If ye love me, keep my commandments for blessed is the man that walketh not in the counsel of ungodly nor standeth in the way of sinners nor sitteth in the seat of the scornful, for His heart is filled with the righteousness of God."

God also had words for those who would not participate service of the Lord. Moses said, "But the man that is clean and is not in a journey, and forbeareth to keep the Passover, even the same soul shall be cut off from among his people. Because he brought not the offering of the Lord in his appointed season, that man shall bear his sin, this where the word validation comes into display. No valid reason for not being there, which is not godly acceptable; there's no reliable fact to support their claim for not being there for if there is something one don't know and living according to the will or God for the scripture, let us know. Ask, and it shall be given you; seek, and ye shall find, knock, and it shall be opened unto you; for every one hat asketh receiveth, and he that seeketh findeth. And to him that knocketh, it shall be opened before going to war."

David asked the Lord concerning war when to go and not to go, and he did as the Lord said, and that was not a specification for David only but whosoever is on the Lord's side is committed to do as he said. We have been bought with a price that we couldn't pay for ourselves but by the blood of Jesus Christ for in that blood left no cloak for sin, no good reason not to be where we should be at the appointed time.

I don't want to be like the man that came to the wedding without the proper attire. And when the king came in to see the guest, he saw there was a man which had not on a wedding garment and he said unto him, "Friend, how commeth thou in hither not having a wedding garment." There is a song that says, "That I had a chance to go to church on Sundays, feet shown with the gospel of truth. Can't do how you want, when you want, and remain in right relationship with the Lord and he was speechless." There is a saying that goes, "If you can't say anything good, it is best to say nothing at all." There was a song of the world that says, "Too late to try again with you. It was too late for the man."

Then the king said to the servants, "Bind his hands and feet and take him and cast him into outer darkness. There shall be weeping and gnashing of teeth." It lets me know that feet must be shown with the gospel of truth. We can't do how we want to when we want to and remain in the right relationship with the Lord; therefore, I don't want to miss anything that involves Jesus Christ not even the suffering because the scripture led us to know in 2 Timothy 2:12, "If we suffer, we shall also reign with him if we deny him he also will deny us." Keeping the appointment is being where one should be at the appointed time for the appointed purpose.

In the parable of the ten virgins, the scripture tells us, "Then shall the kingdom of heaven be likened unto ten virgins which took their lamps and went forth to meet the bridegroom; they all started out in the same purpose and he that overcometh shall inherit all things this relates to the five wise virgins; five of them was foolish, they didn't maintain their right standing in the things of God, he didn't make no one that is beyond his reach as the song says; he can reach way down and pick you up. They that were foolish took their lamps and took no oil with them." It lets us know that our wait for the return of Jesus should not be of a short supply because no one knows the day or the hour when he will return; as one said, be ready, and that is at all times. Then the scripture tells us, "But the wise took oil in their vessels with their lamps they were prepared for a layover, if he doesn't come right now, I will still be ready. While the bridegroom tarried they all slumbered and slept and at midnight there was a cry made, 'Behold, the bridegroom cometh go ye out to meet him.' The wise woke up happy but the foolish is disarray for they had no oil to replenish them, for they said unto the wise, 'Give us of your oil for our lamps are gone out.'"

There are many things we can give of ourselves to others, but this not one of them. You must have this for yourselves that is right standing with the Lord, and it must be before he comes because after the door is shut, no availability is left. As Numbers 9:14 tells us, "And if a stranger shall sojourn among you and will keep the Passover unto the Lord according to the manner thereof so shall he do you shall have same ordinance. Both for the stranger and for

him that was born in the land one law is for everybody."
God has no respecter of person, keep the appointment for
there is another appointment that will be kept, and that is
the appointment of death, and when this body descends,
I want my spirit ascend and be with the Lord for the same
word is for everybody.

The Gift That Keeps on Giving

And it came to pass in those days, that there went out a decree from Caesar Augustus, that all the world should be taxed. (And this taxing was first made when Cyrenius was governor of Syria.) And all went to be taxed, everyone into his own city. And Joseph also went up from Galilee, out of the city of Nazareth, into Judaea, unto the city of David, which is called Bethlehem; (because he was of the house and lineage of David:) To be taxed with Mary his espoused wife, being great with child. And so it was, that, while they were there, the days were accomplished that she should be delivered. And she brought forth her firstborn son, and wrapped him in swaddling clothes, and laid him in a manger; because there was no room for them in the inn. A manger; because there was no room for them in the inn. (Luke 2:1–7)

Now when they heard this they pricket in their hearts, and said unto Peter and to the rest of the apostles, "Men and brethren, what shall we do?" Then Peter said unto them, "Repent, and be baptized every one of you in the name of Jesus Christ for the remission of sins and ye shall receive the gift of the Holy Ghost for the promise is unto you, and to your children, and to all that are afar off even as many as the Lord our God shall call and with many others. Words did he testify and exhort, saying save yourselves from this untoward generation, then they that gladly received his word were baptized." And the same day there were added unto them about three thousand souls. (Acts 2:37–41)

T his gift can be shared with others, and the one that do the sharing still have it all! For you see, when man gives a gift, he is left void of the gift, but when God gives a gift, there is no lacking. The gift that man gives, the person's name is written on it, but the gift that God gave, whosoever will let them come. The gift that man gives sooner or later is all used up, but the gift that God gave is eternal. Not the lights in the streets, but the light in the heart for you see, when celebrating a person's birthday, it includes the involvement of the person, and as the saying goes, "Jesus is the reason for the season."

The scripture in Matthew tells us that an angel of the Lord appeared unto Joseph. "Thou son of David, fear not to take unto thee Mary thy wife, for that which is conceived in her is of the Holy Ghost. The word that was with God and the word was God is now planted in the matrix of a virgin named Mary." In all other cares except for Adam and Eve, it took male and female to produce a child, and life begins after his birth. But Jesus existed before his birth in the form of the word for the scripture let us know, "And the word was made flesh and dwelt among us and we beheld his glory." The glory as the only begotten Son of the father full of grace and truth. The gift that keep on giving.

Luke tells us, "And it came to pass in those days, that there went out a decree from Caesar Augustus, that all the world should be taxed." To everything, there is season and a time to every purpose under the heaven. God's plan was coming into motion at the right time and at the right place. And this taxing was made when Cyrenius was governor of Syria, and all went to be taxed, everyone into his own city, and Joseph also went up from Galilee out of the city of Nazareth into Judea unto the city of David, which is called Bethlehem. Because he was of the house and lineage of David, God used the stage that was set by man. Man's intention was to count all the people so he would know how many belong to him for the purpose of taxation, but it was God's intention to show that people everywhere belongs to no one but him. Being obedient to this decree, Joseph and his espoused wife Mary near the end of her being with child made the trip. There was no room for them in the inn, so they were assigned to a stable, and that's where "silent night, holy night" began. There's never a night like this before and never will be again.

God knew Censure took place. Jesus in his adult life said render therefore Caesar the things that is of Caesar's and unto God the things which be of God. That is our hearts, and as the song says, "Go tell it on the mountain over the hills and everywhere, that Jesus Christ is born." Holy is God in the fashion of men, the only one that has two histories. God and man the Holy Spirit brought deity and humanity in one person for the purpose of bringing Christ likewise into our character. The gift that keeps on giving, which can be shared with others and still have it all.

I can understand the one that Jesus healed and told him not to tell nobody but he went and spread it much. For you see, when you have been touched by Jesus, you got to tell somebody as the song says, "Can't keep it to myself when I get my Social Security check." When this one and that one get their share, there is little to none left, but I can share Jesus with the whole wide world and still have him all!

The scripture in Acts tells us, "Now when they heard this, they were pricked in their hearts, and said unto Peter and the rest of the apostles, 'Men and brethren, what shall we do?'" It lets us know that what shall we do in time is still at hand. And the answer is always the same: repent and be baptized in the name of Jesus Christ for the remission of sin. Without repentance and turning away, there is no celebration of his birth without a new birth of one's self. It lets us know that some took heed for unto them were added about three thousand souls membership; without Christ membership is to no avail for it must be about a new way of life.

Christmas is not about the lights that plug in the socket, but the light that is in the heart which have been lit up by Jesus Christ. For he is the light of the world and all else is darkness for he is the gift that keeps on giving, and it is not just for a chosen few but whosoever will let them come. He is not an individual gift but one that can be shared with all. While Paul and Silas were locked in jail with their feet in shackles, at midnight, they prayed and sang praises unto God, and the prisoners heard them. Suddenly, there was a great earthquake so that the foundation of the prison was shaken.

There is a song of the world that says, "The jailhouse rock." God rocked the jailhouse. There is no divine limit that God won't do for those of his people. The doors were opened, and everyone's bands were loosening, not for the purpose of escape but a chance for somebody to know who Jesus is. As a result, the keeper of the prison cried out, "What must I do to be saved?" And the result was not only himself but all his household, letting us know there is still a chance with Jesus. The scripture tells us that the child Samuel heard a voice calling him three times, and he thought it was Eli, but Eli let him know that if he heard the voice again, he must say, "Speak, Lord, for your servant is listening."

All who have not commit, what a testimony that would be on the day of the celebration of the birth of Jesus who a new birth of one's self that is to be born from above. When the joy of Christmas has fade away, the joy of Jesus will remain. When he was asked by the Jews, "Are thou greater than our father Abraham?" He let them know, "Before Abraham was I am. Before the day was I am. There is no other that can deliver out of my hand; I will work and who shall let it." Abraham was the head of the Jewish race, and Jesus is the head of eternal life. He is greater than the temple of the center of worship. Church membership without Jesus center ship is of no avail.

Jesus is greater than Solomon in the excellence of his wisdom and wealth. To turn away from God, these things are of no avail. He was greater than Jonah who was against God blessing the Gentiles. Christ came not to call the righteous but sinners to repent. He is greater than Jacob who gave his people a well; Jesus provided all who are his rivers of living water. Man was born innocent and became a sinner; Jesus was born holy and remain holy. Adam was the head of the human race. Jesus is the head of the spiritual race. One came out of the dust and the other the spirit that will never die.

God blessed man with different talents to supply the needs of one another. When you need to hear good singing, you can call on Sister Teresa and Sister Sandra. When you need help with your income taxes, you can call on brother Zeb. When you need your lawn mower fix, you can call on brother Sumpter. If you need a deck built, you can call on brother Timothy. But for the saving of the soul, you got to call on Jesus! There are different things people like to link with to make themselves feel important, but the best of them all is to be linked with Jesus Christ. Some in the church of Corinthian had the thought pattern that I am of Paul, I am of Apollos, but the best of I am is of Jesus Christ for by no other name can one inter into eternal rest.

Adam was the head of the human race, and Jesus is the head of the spiritual race; one came out of the dust, the other by the spirit; one was made innocent and became sinner and one was born holy and remain holy.

I can understand why the song writer wrote "Joy to the world the Lord is come." For what he is going to do? As the birth of a child, it brings joy to the parents, but the birth of Jesus brings joy to the whole world. Upon accepting of who he is, which is of disarray, can made to become into the right order that is everything that is unfixed. Jesus can bring it into the right spiritually and sometime from the natural for he said to the man with the withered hand, "Stretch forth thine hand; and he stretched it forth and it was restored as the other." The true celebration of Christmas is those who have stretched forth their life and the birth of Jesus is on the inside, no longer of one's self but a new creature.

Then we can sing with a true heart, "Joy to the world the Lord is come let earth receive her king. Let every heart receive her king." I received my king.

My grandson Alex was very smart in school, and upon graduation, he received a lifetime scholarship. My goal is to achieve a lifetime citizenship in the kingdom of God!

Learning the Full Scope of Jesus

> In the beginning was the Word, and the Word was with God, and the Word was God. The same was in the beginning with God. All things were made by him; and without him was not anything made that was made. In him was life; and the life was the light of men. And the light shineth in darkness; and the darkness comprehended it not. There was a man sent from God, whose name was John. The same came for a witness, to bear witness of the Light, that all men through him might believe. He was not that Light, but was sent to bear witness of that Light. That was the true Light, which lighteth every man that cometh into the world. He was in the world, and the world was made by him, and the world knew him not. (1 John 1:1– 10)

Not just that he came into the world but that he was also there before there was a world, the life of men, and all other living creature began with birth. But not with Jesus for the in the scripture of John, it lets us know there is more to Jesus before he was conceived of the Holy Ghost for it tells us in the beginning was the word and the word was with God and the word was God before he created the world.

Jesus said that when his hour had come to leave this world, "and now, Father, glorify thou me with thine own self with the glory which I had with thee before the world was." It lets me know that he was there all the time even before the beginning of time as we know it with man's time staled with the creation but not with Jesus. That's why I'm going to hold to Jesus no matter what comes and what does not come because in him comes that which no one else can give. For he said, "I am come that thy might have life," and they might have it more abundantly one of the things that the world didn't give and the world can't take away for there is no misjudgments in Jesus Christ for he is the one that gets it right all the time. The same was in the beginning, there is no before time, and it was not Jesus. When God created the heaven and the earth, Jesus was there; he is the word that brought it into being. The next verse tell us that all things were made by him, and without him there was not anything made that was made.

There are many honor in life that mankind can achieve, but the greatest of them all is to be connected to the one that made everything. For the eyes of the Lord are upon the righteous, and his ears are open unto their cry. You see, what Jesus did is not just which is written in the red but that also which is written in the black for the next verse tells us that in him was life and the life was the light of men. Even if we acknowledge him or not, our destination will be determined by Jesus for he said, "I am the light of the world he that followeth me shall not walk in the darkness, but shall have the light of life." Light and darkness cannot exist together; it's either the one or the other, letting me know to stay steadfast and unmovable, always abiding in the works of the Lord.

There was a man sent from God whose name was John, the same came for to bear witness of the light that all men through him might believe the one that when his mother Elizabeth heard the salutation of Mary, the babe leaped in her womb. We live in a world of disarray, but when we think of all the goodness of Jesus and all that he is doing for us, we, too, leap for joy for greater is he that is within me than he that is in the world. The joy of the Lord is our strength, and in this, we know that weeping may endure for a night, but joy will come in the morning and not just joy but unspeakable joy that is beyond the thought pattern. I don't know yet the full scope of Jesus for Jesus said through the Apostle Paul, "For now we see through a glass darkly, but then face to face man. Now I know in part; but then shall I know even as also I am known." Paul said, 'I know in part, which mean some but not all of a thing." For again he said, "I press toward the mark for the prize of the high calling of God in Christ Jesus." It lets me know we walk in the way of righteousness; there is a prize to be received and that is eternal life with Jesus, and who in their right mind wouldn't want this inducted in their life?

John said that he was not that light but was sent to bear witness of the light, letting me know that there is something about Jesus that cannot be provided by no one else. All John could say, and we can also say, that Jesus is true light which lights every man that come into the world. It had already been said in Isaiah 49:6, "It is a light thing that thou shouldest be my servant to raise up the tribes of Jacob and to restore the preserved of Israel; I will also give thee for a light to the Gentiles, that thou mayest be my salvation unto the end of the earth." He was in the world, and the world was made by him, and the world knew him not. He came unto his own, and his own received him not. The ones that Moses said, "The Lord thy God will raise up unto thee a prophet from the midst of thee. Of thy brethren like unto me, unto him thy shall harken." And again God said, "I will put my words in his mouth, and he shall speak unto them all that I commanded him." The Father is talking about Jesus while still in the form of the word of his mission when he comes in the flesh. I have heard one said, "I ask you, Lord, but I won't beg," but the scripture lets us to know that this poor man cried, and the Lord heard him and saved him out of all his troubles. Again the scripture lets us know that even though there's as many advancements in life that have features of being good, the best of them all is to have the label as being a child of God which identifies the owner of one person I know that you are a Christion without your mouth being opened.

In 1 Peter 4:2, it said, "He no longer should live the rest of his time in the flesh to the lust of man, but to the will of God." Happy is the people that is in such a case; yes, happy is that people whose God is their Lord. Then it tells us how he was born, which is not of blood or of the will of the flesh or of the will of man but of God. It lets me know that in order to become a child of God, I must go through a supernatural birth, one that which is born of flesh is flesh and that which is born of spirit is spirit for flesh and blood cannot enter into the kingdom of God. There is a slogan of the military, "Be all you can be," but in this, "Be none of you except that it be according to the will of God." No longer of one's self but has been bought by the precious blood of Christ Jesus; no longer do as I please but that which pleases the Lord with gladness of the heart.

In the scripture in John tells us, "And the word was made flesh, and dwell among us and we beheld his glory the glory as of the only begotten Son of the father full of grace and truth." It lets us know that he existed before he was of the flesh, before he became flesh. Jesus said of his own self,

"Listen, disciples, unto me and hearken ye people for the Lord hath called me from the wombs; from the bowels of my mother hath he made mention of my name. Joseph thou son of David fear not to take unto thee Mary thy wife for that which is conceived in her is of the Holy Ghost, and she shall bring forth a son and thou shalt call his name Jesus for he shall save his people from their sins." And again Jesus said, "And he hath made my mouth like a sharp sword in the shadow of his hand hath he hid me, and made me a polished shaft in his quiver, hath he hid me."

The first five verses of Isaiah chapter 49, Jesus is speaking of himself and his mission before he was born. You see, there is so much about Jesus; one can't tell it all in one sitting, neither in one's lifetime. The scripture lets us know that when the fullness of the time has come, God sent his son; made of a women made under the law. As the song said, "He was there all the time, waiting in line to redeem them that were under the law, that we might receive the adoption of sons no longer on the outside but on the inside of the righteousness of God." Jesus did that for man could do for himself for he said, "I am the way, the truth, and the life; no man cometh unto the father but by me."

There are so many wonderful things about Jesus I can't tell them all. There are some that use the title of Lord before their name or the office, such as Lord Barron, but Jesus is Lord of lords. King David was a king after God's own heart, but Jesus is King of kings for David said, "And in the days of these kings shall the God of heaven set up a kingdom which shall never be destroyed and the kingdom shall not be left to other people, but it shall break in pieces and consume all these kingdom, and it shall stand forever, the one that Jesus will establish and I myself want to be of that kingdom, that's why I'm going to do what Jesus saith." As the saying goes, "If he saith to jump, 'Not why, Lord,' but 'How high you want me to jump?'" Paul tells us in Galatians 3:13, "Christ hath redeemed us from the curse of the land, being made a curse for us for it is written cursed is everyone that hangeth on a tree."

"For unto you is born this day in the city of David a savior which is Christ the Lord" (Luke 2:22). "Who his own self has bare our sins in his body on the tree that we become dead to sin should live unto righteousness by whose stripes ye were healed" (1 Pet. 2:24).

Solomon way back then said his mouth is most sweet. "Yeah, he is altogether lovely, this my beloved and this is my friend, oh daughters of Jerusalem." David said, "Until the ancient of days come, and the judgment was given to saints of the Most High and the time come that the saints possessed the kingdom." Paul said in Hebrews 12:3, "Looking unto Jesus the author and finisher of our faith who for the joy that was not before him and used cross, despising the shame and is set down at the right hand of the throne of God for he is the author of eternal salvation." He is the one that made it possible. There are many things in life that one can do without, but Jesus is not one of them whether one believe him or not, it still takes Jesus to sustain. I have heard people said on the outside of Christ, on the outside of his divine will, yes, for David said, "Whither shall I go from thy spirit or whither shall I flee from thy presence." Jesus has the last say whether one is for or against him. The scripture in Colossians tells us, "For it pleased the Father that's in him." Jesus should all fullness dwell all things stays in its rightful place.

For everything that God made stayed within the purpose for which it was created: the earth stayed in its right orbit, the sun to shine in the daytime, the moon and stars by night for the lesser light of night, the water in its boundary, man for the purpose of worship. Israel wanted a God that they could see. Jesus is the God that we can see, and he have made peace through the blood of his cross, by him to reconcile all things unto himself, by him I say, whether they are things in earth or things in heaven, things didn't stay in their created order. Sin had separate us from God, and we need to be reconciled to bring things back into the right order.

Job spoke of needing someone to mediate between him and God, someone who understood what he was going through. Jesus as man understood our situation, and since he is God, he can fix them all, whatever the need might be. Therefore, if any man be in Christ Jesus—he is a new creature—old things are passed away. Behold all things become new. Here I am, Lord. Use me for your benefit for I'm standing in the promises of the Lord. He that believeth in me shall not perish but shall have eternal life, bearing of the full scope of Jesus, no longer alienated and enemies in the mind by wicked works yet now both be reconciled, who was dead in trespasses and sins are now alive in Jesus Christ who is eternal life. In that of his flesh through death, he presents us holy and blameless and proven in his sight being perfect for I am perfect; therefore, Jesus cannot speak in contrary if you continue in the faith grounded and settled and not be moved away from the hope of the gospel, which you have heard and which was preached to every creature which is under heaven.

God has done his part that which is left is for man to do. A right relationship with God has a twofold purpose, God points the way and man follow. How can two walk together except they agree? So, therefore, the answer is yes Jesus to your will and your way. It is an ongoing thing because we don't know yet all there is to Jesus. John said, "Jesus said, 'I am that bread of life.'" Luke said, "God hath raised up a horn of salvation for us in the house of his servant David." And again Paul said, "He is the Lord of glory."

Again I say all about Jesus cannot be told in one sitting. First John said, "Behold now are we the sons of God, and it doth not appear what we shall be like, but we know that, when he shall appear, we shall be like him; for we shall see him as he is." What a conclusion that will be to see him as he is everything in life may not be worthwhile, but this one is.

Being of the Brotherhood

Therefore whosoever heareth these sayings of mine, and doeth them, I will liken him unto a wise man, which built his house upon a rock: And the rain descended, and the floods came, and the winds blew, and beat upon that house; and it fell not: for it was founded upon a rock. And everyone that heareth these sayings of mine, and doeth them not, shall be likened unto a foolish man, which built his house upon the sand: And the rain descended, and the floods came, and the winds blew, and beat upon that house; and it fell: and great was the fall of it. And it came to pass, when Jesus had ended these sayings, the people were astonished at his doctrine: For he taught them as one having authority, and not as the scribes. (Matt. 7:24–29)

There came then his brethren and his mother, and, standing without, sent unto him, calling him. And the multitude sat about him, and they said unto him, "Behold, thy mother and thy brethren without seek for thee." And he answered them saying who is my mother, or my brethren: and he looked round about on them which sat about him, and said, "Behold my mother and my brethren for whosoever shall do the will of God, the same is my brother, and my sister, and mother." (Mark 3:31– 35)

In this thing that didn't work beforehand will work now for it get rid of the things that I used to do and replace them with the things that I should be doing. Being of the brotherhood is growing power, growing out of the things that which should not be into the things that which should be, leaving which is contrary to the will of God and having that which brings about life eternal, the death of old self, and a new beginning.

The scripture in Matthew tells us about two builders, one was wise and the other foolish for Jesus said, "Therefore whosoever hears these sayings of mine and doeth them is like a wise man who built his house on a rock." He said unto Simon, whom he later named Peter, "Launch out into the deep and let down your nets for drought." And Simon, answering, said unto him, "Master, we have toiled all the night, and have taken nothing nevertheless at thy word I will let down the net." When they had this done, they enclosed a great multitude of fish to the point that their net broke. Oh, what a difference a Christ- ordained life makes. I will liken unto a wise man which built his house upon a rock; a rock is a hard foundation, a firm and dependable support, protection from the source of danger and destruction, the choosing of spiritual life over spiritual death. That rock is Jesus Christ, and then he tells us as the rain descended and the flood came and the winds blow and beat upon the house, it fell not. A life that is connected to Jesus can take a licking and keep on kicking for it was founded upon a rock "for the foundation of God standeth sure, and everyone that heareth these saying of mine and doeth them not shall be likened unto a foolish man which built his home upon the sand."

It had a boomerang effect which went contrary to his expectation, not only must one hear the word for the scripture tell us, but "be ye doers of my word and not hearers, only deceiving your own selves." The foolish man thought he could get by with the hearing and not the doing, and, therefore, he took shortcuts and built his house upon the sand. We are living in a time of inflation, and shortcuts are needed; we can't have bacon with my grits, but with the word of God, no shortcut is allowed. The foolish man thought he could have it all without doing it all; therefore, he built his house upon the sand, but sand has no stability; when the wind blows, there it goes. Then Jesus tells us, "And the rain descended and the flood came and winds blow and beat upon that house, and it fell and great was the fall of it." It lets me know to stay under God's umbrella which provides protection for life present and that which to come.

The word of God hast a twofold purpose: hear the word and do the word, and he doesn't ask a thing without giving the ability to perform it. When Jesus asked his disciples, "Whom do man say that I the Son of Man am?" And Simon Peter assured and said, "Thou are the Christ, the son of the living God for it was made available unto him." As David said, "Thy word have I hid in mine heart, that I might not sin against thee." It lets us know that which is contrary presents itself. It can be blocked with the word of God for man live not by bread alone but by every word that proceeds out of the mouth of God, and in his word is some dos and don'ts. I have heard one said, "If you stay in the dos, there won't be any time left for the don'ts for God doesn't ask a thing without giving the ability to perform it. And Jesus makes it plain, and it come to pass.

When Jesus had ended these sayings, the people were astonished at his doctrine for he taught them as one having authority and not as the scribes, never was a man like this man before. The scripture in John tells us, "Then came the officers to the chief priests and the Pharisees; and they said unto them, 'Why have ye not brought him?' The officers answered, 'Never a man spoke like this man.'" Because there was never a man like this before. A songwriter said, "Tossing and turning, I couldn't sleep at all last night, but the scripture said, "Be careful for nothing but in everything in prayer and supplication with thanksgiving. Let your request be known unto God, and the peace of God, which passes all understanding, shall keep your hearts and minds through Christ Jesus." And another songwriter said, "My soul just couldn't rest contented until I found the Lord not complete within one self." Again the scripture tells us, "For ye are bought with a price, therefore glorify God in your body, and in your spirit which are God's."

I can say like David, I will bless the Lord at all times; his praise shall continually be in my mouth, looking not to the things which are temporal but those that everlasting. When being in the right place with God, one ask if he will make it possible for this is the possibility to know what to ask of him and what to refrain from. Jesus said, "If ye then, being evil, know how to give good gift to your children, how much more shall your father which is in heaven give good things to them that ask him?" And it tells us, "He that hath pity upon the poor lendeth unto the Lord; and that which he hath given will God pay him again, being of the brotherhood."

The scripture in Mark tells us, "There come then his brethren and his mother and standing without sent unto him calling him." For what purpose, the scripture did not say, and the multitude was about him, and they said unto him, "Behold thy mother and thy brethren without seek for thee." And he answered them saying, "Who is my mother or my brethren?" He left the physical location and went into the spiritual. And he looked round about on them which sat about him and said, "Behold my mother and my brethren."

As the song said, "We are family, my sister and my brothers." It is not a bloodline but of the well of water springing up into everlasting life. No longer as the certain ruler asked him saying, "Good Master, what shall I do to inherit eternal life?" Jesus has rung out the old and ringing in the new, rung out the false and ringing in the true, not that I have already attained, but I press toward the mark for the prize of the high calling of God in Christ Jesus. Not that I know everything, but I follow hard after that which is to be known for he said, "Walk before me and be perfect." God doesn't ask a thing if it cannot be done. Because he gives the ability also, and when opposition comes greater, it's he that is in me than he that is in the world.

I can say like Isaiah, "And he that made my mouth like a sharp sword in the shadow of his hand hath he hid me, and made me a polished shaft; in his quiver hath he hid me." No longer is the resource less for he will supply all our needs according to his riches in glory being in the brotherhood. There is a song that said, "We are family, my sisters, and my brothers and me." It's not a bloodline but a Christ- line. "Behold what manner of love the father hath bestowed upon us that we be called sons of God and doth not yet appear what we shall be known that when he shall appear, we shall be like him." We shall see him as he is, no longer looking through a glass darkly but then face to face for it is good to be for Jesus, even better to be with Jesus being of the brotherhood.

The Eight Words of Jonah

And the word of the Lord came unto Jonah the second time, saying, "Arise, go unto Nineveh, that great city, and preach unto it the preaching that I bid thee." So Jonah arose, and went unto Nineveh, according to the word of the Lord. Now Nineveh was an exceeding great city of three days' journey. And Jonah began to enter into the city a day's journey, and he cried, and said, "Yet forty days, and Nineveh shall be overthrown." So the people of Nineveh believed God, and proclaimed a fast, and put on sackcloth, from the greatest of them even to the least of them. For word came unto the king of Nineveh, and he arose from his throne, and he laid his robe from him, and covered him with sackcloth, and sat in ashes. And he caused it to be proclaimed and published through Nineveh by the decree of the king and his nobles, saying, "Let neither man nor beast, herd nor flock, taste any thing: let them not feed, nor drink water: But let man and beast be covered with sackcloth, and cry mightily unto God: yea, let them turn everyone from his evil way, and from the violence that is in their hands. Who can tell if God will turn and repent, and turn away from his fierce anger, that we perish not?" And God saw their works, that they turned from their evil way; and God repented of the evil, that he had said that he would do unto them; and he did it not. (Jon. 3)

The scripture tells us the second time, letting us know that there was a time that was before the second time; the first time one did not take heed, and if God did not intend for a person to do a thing, he would not have assigned to their hands. There are many things in life for man to do, but being disobedient to God is not one of them! Jonah had to find out the hard way, the result for not complying to the will of God. There are many things in life that mankind can say no to, but not to God. When God say yes, King David found out the hard way, the result for not complying to the will of God. The scripture tells us that when the kings go forth to battle, David tarried still at Jerusalem. For when one is where they should be, it eliminates the probability of that which should not happen from happening. He would not have been exposed to the circumstances that caused him to sin. When fully committed to the will of God, it blocks out all that is contrary. The scene of a woman bathing herself would have been avoided, and the result of what happen would have never taken place. But David didn't stay under these circumstances, he wanted the Lord to take full control of his life, with none of him left to himself for he said, "Purge me with hyssop and I shall be clean, wash me, and I shall be whiter than snow." He wanted the Lord to purge out— therefore the old leaven—that he may be a new lump. And one of the result is that one will be where they should be at the appointed time.

Back in the mule and wagon, days and the time when we lived in a house that was really close to a dirt road, we played a game. Knowing when the wagon was empty, all you could hear was rattling, but when it was full, all you could hear was the huff of the mule hitting the dirt road.

David said, "Create in me a clean heal, oh God, and renew a right spirit within me for all else is just a lot of noise." David had experienced what a sin life was all about, and he didn't want that to continue for a life separated from

God is no life at all! All the benefits that comes with a God-ordained life is missing, leaving a void of dissentient. There is a saying, "Wake up and smell the coffee"; no more void of God in his life.

One of the needs that God suspended upon mankind is the need for his presence, food for the natural body, and a right relationship for the soul as the Lord shut Noah in before the flood. David wanted to be shut in with the Lord. No room left for which is contrary, nothing that can transcend which is not of God. When you do this for me, Lord, I won't keep it to myself, then will I teach transgression your way and sinners shall be converted unto thee. Unlike Jonah, the one that God told "arise, go to Nineveh that great city and cry against it for their wickedness is come up before me," perhaps he thought that the God of Israel should not be the God of no one else, but I have news for you, Jonah, the more you share him is the proof of the more you have him. But Jonah had to learn when God says, "Yes, who am I to say no?" Jonah had to learn you can't do some of God and left some, but while in the belly of a fish, Jonah learned that one can't say no to God when God says yes without consequences.

As John the Baptist said, "And think not within yourselves, we have Abraham to our father for I say unto you that God is able of these stones to raise up children unto Abram. But God is a God of another chance."

After Jonah repented and back on dry land, the word of the Lord came unto Jonah the second time, saying, "Arise, go unto Nineveh that great city and preach unto it the preaching that I bid thee." I have heard people said "Get your groove on," "get with the program," "get into that which you should be doing," so Jonah arose and went unto Nineveh according to the word of the Lord. As David said, "Thy word is a lamp unto my feet, and a light unto my path". And God wanted this for all people.

Now Nineveh was an exceeding great city of three days' journey. Three days from where Jonah was, but when you are traveling for the Lord, distance doesn't matter. Jesus traveled through forty and two generations to save man from their sin, and Jonah began to enter into the city a day's journey and he cried and said, yet forty days and Nineveh shall be overturn. The eight words of Jonah, some have been having the word of God with many words and many years and still won't turn to the Lord. For Jesus said, "The men of Nineveh shall rise up in judgment with this generation and shall condemn it because they repented at the preaching of Jonah." Behold a greater man than Jonah is here for he said, "I am the vine and ye are branches, he that abideth in me and I in him the same bringeth forth much fruit for without me ye can do nothing."

If the people of Nineveh believed God and proclaimed a fast and put on sackcloth from the greatest of them even to the least of them, no more is said about what Jonah said for the king took over, arose from his throne, and laid his robe from him and covered himself with sackcloth and sat in ashes. The king didn't wait until the forty days had expired. He took it as a right thing. God is upon all them for good that seek him, and it also lets us know that tomorrow is not a promise to you today. Sackcloth and ashes are representation of humility for the scripture let us know.

The Pharisees stood and prayed thus with himself. "God, I thank thee, that I am not as other men are, extortions, unjust, adulterers, or even as the publicans, I fast twice in the week. I give tithes of all that I possess." And the publican standing afar off would not lift up so much as his eyes unto heaven but smote upon his breast, saying, "God, be merciful to me a sinner." I tell you this man went down to his house justified rather than the other for everyone that exalted himself shall be abased; and he that humbled himself shall be exalted for God resisted the proud but give grace to the humble. Not only did the king did this himself, but he also cause it to be proclaimed and published through Nineveh by the decree of the king and his nobles saying, "Let neither man nor beast, herd nor flock, taste anything, let the man not feed nor drink water."

As David said, "Let everything that hath breath praise the Lord; for when praises goes up, blessings comes down, but let men and beast be covered with sackcloth and cry mightily unto God yea let them turn everyone from his evil way and from the violence that is in their hands." You see, we serve a "you do and I will" God for the word of God tells us let the wicked forsake his way and the unrighteous man his thoughts and let him return unto the Lord and he will have mercy upon him and to our God. He will abundantly pardon if you don't relent but repent; you have a place with God, and the result is as David said, "I will bless the Lord at all times, and his praises shall continually be in my mouth." There's no space left for which is contrary. Who can tell if God will turn and repent and turn away his fierce anger that we perish not? For again the word of God said, "He that covereth his sins shall not prosper but who so confesseth and forsaketh shall have mercy." As David said, "I will bless the Lord at all times, and his praises shall always be in my mouth." It eliminates which is contrary.

Being in the right relationship with God is a sure foundation, and God saw their work that they turned from their evil way, and God repented of the evil that he had said he would do unto them and he did it not. I have heard one said, "I will go even if I have to go by myself," but you don't have to go by yourself, I'll go. As David said, "I'd rather be a doorkeeper in the house of the Lord than to dwell in the tent of wickedness." All are not great pretenders for John said after this, "I beheld and a great multitude which no man could number, of all nations and kindred and people, and tongues stood before the throne and before the lamb, clothed with white robes and palms in their hands."

Somebody is doing what Jesus said. As the song said, "Oh, how I got over, many are going to make it over." For Jesus said, "Therefore whosoever heareth these saying of mine, an doeth them, I will liken him unto a wise man, winch built his house upon a rock and the rain descended and the flood came, and the winds blew, and beat upon that house and it fell not; for it was founded upon a rock." It lets me know that when you do what Jesus said, there is no undesirable side effects. Everything invents itself. God takes it away when you do what Jesus said for this is the love of God, that we keep His commandments, and his commandments are not grievous.

If eight words from Jonah caused Nineveh to turn to the Lord, let us consider what the many words of Jesus can do for us. Lazarus had been dead for four long days, but Jesus said, "Lazarus, come forth," and Lazarus came forth. He made a little clay and put it on the eyes of the man that was born blind and said, "Go wash," and the man receiveth his sight. There was a man that had been in his condition thirty and eight long years. Jesus said unto him, "Take up thy bed and walk." He took up his bed and he walked.

When I had a sewing shop in West Columbia, there was a room I used for a praying room. One day while on my knees in that room, Jesus said, "Get up of your knees and do what I told you to do for you don't know what you can do when you haven't tried. Go tell my people I love them."

I Thought He Was
Talking About Me

That night the king could not sleep, and he commanded to bring the book of records of the chronicles, and they were read before the king. And it was found written that Mordecai had told of Bigthana and Teresh, two of the king's chamberlains, the keepers of the door, who sought to lay hand on the King Ahasuerus. And the king said, "What honor and dignity hath been done to Mordecai for this?" Then the king's servants that ministered unto him said, "There is nothing done for him." And the king said, "Who is in the court?" Now Haman was come into the outward court of the king's house to speak unto the king to hang Mordecai on the gallows that he had prepared for him. And the king's servants said unto him, "Behold, Haman standeth in the court." And the king said, "Let him come in." So Haman came in. And the king said unto him, "What shall be done unto the man whom the king delighteth to honor?" Now Haman thought in his heart, *To whom would the king delight to do honor more than to myself?* And Haman answered the king, "For the man whom the king delighteth to honor, let the royal apparel be brought which the king useth to wear, and the horse that the king rideth upon, and the crown royal which is set upon his head: And let this apparel and horse be delivered to the hand of one of the king's most noble princes, that they may array the man withal whom the king delighteth to honor, and bring him on horseback through the street of the city, and proclaim before him, Thus shall it be done to the man whom the king delighteth to honor." Then the king said to Haman, "Make haste, and take the apparel and the horse, as thou hast said, and do even so to Mordecai the Jew, that sitteth at the king's gate: let nothing fail of all that thou hast spoken." (Esther 6:1–10)

"I Thought He Was Talking About Me" is wanting that is good for one's self and evil for others, which is one of the greatest letdown in life and in this case call for a death sentence. Proverb 10:21 tells us, "Death and life are in the power of the tongue, and they that love it shall eat the fruit thereof."

What you say means life or death; those who love to talk will be rewarded for what they say. The scripture in Esther tells us that King Ahasuerus had trouble sleeping; there was something in his consciousness that had to be resolved, a sign that God was at work even thought his name is not mentioned anywhere in the book of Esther for he is a lifesaving God and this thing is worldwide.

The king asked that the official record books be brought to him; while it was read to him, he came upon where it was written to assassinate him, and because of Mordecai, the plot was exposed and dealt with, He wanted to know if any honor was given for his loyalty. He was told that nothing had been done. The scripture lets us know that Haman arrived at the scene to ask the king permission to hang Mordecai. As the song said, "He is an on-time God, yes, he is."

God had already set up for Mordecai that would be no hanging for him but blessings. As Balaam let Balak know who can curse whom God has blessed, he didn't get a chance to tell the king his purpose for being there. For the king asked him what shall be done unto the man whom the king delighted to honor. It came into his thought pattern that he was the one that the king wanted to honor, "I thought he was talking about me." He came with a grand scheme. The man is to be dressed in royal apparel, the royal crown upon his head, riding through the city on the king horse, by one of the king's most noble princes, who will announce that the one riding on the horse is being especially honored by the king. The king accepted Haman's suggestion but then came the letdown as he heard it being said, letting the air out of one's tire. He learned that the one to be honored is Mordecai; you're talking about a double whammy, this is one of them. The one who came to the king for the purpose of hanging was going to be honored by the king and appointed him to carry it out; which he wanted for himself was given to the man that he wanted dead just because he would not bow down to him.

When Peter went to meet Cornelius, he met Peter and fell down at his feet and worshipped him, but Peter took him up, saying, "Stand up. I myself also a man." It lets us know who is in charge of the events of life, not Haman but God. There is a song that said, "Lord, if I get too high, bring me down." But that is one thing we don't have to ask the Lord for if we get too high; he will bring us down. Or what a difference being a child of God makes Haman's plan backfired on him. It was a turnaround of events, which he had purpose in his heart. The one that was in sackcloth is now in a royal robe.

They that wait upon the Lord shall renew their strength; they shall mount up with wings as eagles, they shall run and not be weary, and they shall walk and faint not. But he could have known for the invisible things of him from the creation of the world are clearly seen, being understood by the things that are made even his eternal power and godhead so they are without excuse.

You see, the Jews weren't the only people that could be in a right relationship with God even back then because Noah was a righteous man before there was a Jew. It lets me know that whosoever will let them come is not just a now thing but a then also. But Haman had a high look which prevented him to know what the effects of righteousness was all about, that "blessed is the man who walketh not in the counsel of the ungodly and not that only nor standeth in the way of sinners nor sitteth in the seat of the scornful."

Jesus said unto the lame man at the pool of Bethesda, "Wilt thou be made whole." He Had been made whole not by works of righteousness which we have done but according to his mercy. He saved us by the washing of regeneration and renewing of the Holy Ghost, and the result is to delight in the law of the Lord, and in his law does he meditates day and night. I have heard one said, "It takes the word to save us, and it takes the word to keep us save." Just as it takes physical food daily to keep the flesh body alive, it takes spiritual food daily to keep the spiritual conscience in focus, and the result is "he shall be like a tree planted the rivers of water that bringeth forth his fruit in its season and fruit in that which of righteousness." And it is also said his leaf shall not wither.

When that which is contrary comes, don't cause one to be less committed. There is no time spent halting between two opinions for God is God, and the flowering is of them at all times. As David said, "I was glad when they said unto me let us go into the house of the Lord." For being in the house of the Lord is not just to be in worship service but enclosed in righteousness at all times. The ungodly are not so as the

Psalm said, "Who may stand in thy sight when once thou be angry." It won't be the ungodly, but it's like separating the grain from the husk, the good fell to the ground and the chaff blew away in wind. Some of you know how we used to do it. Therefore, the ungodly shall not stand in the judgment. Let us know in the time of reckoning some choosing must be made for there is an ending result, a separation will take place one where God is and the other is where he is not.

Paul said to be absent from the body is to be present with the Lord, but not in all cases it is a place for the righteous and a place for the ungodly. And as the saying goes "You can fool man some of the time, but you can't fool God none of the time" for the Lord knows the way of the righteous, but the way of the ungodly shall perish, and everything that God does is not slack. No one that is righteous will end in the place with the ungodly, and no one that is ungodly will end up in the place of the righteous. The scripture tells us, "For now we see through a glass darkly." We may not get it right all the time, but God gets it right all the time. Again Paul said, "Not as though I had already attained either were already perfect, but I follow after if that I may apprehend that for which also I am apprehended of Christ Jesus."

It is a growing process of staying in the will of God, and not just in his will but reaching a higher height and a deeper depth for it wards off that which is contrary to the will of God. When King Ahasuerus said unto Haman "What shall be done unto the man whom the king delighteth to honor," he thought the king was talking about him. But when Jesus said "Come unto me all ye that labor and are heavy laden and I will give rest," I know that he was talking to me. It is said if you overload the current that comes into your house, the breakers will trip, but you can overload your troubles on Jesus and the circuit will not be broken. For he said, "Take my yoke upon you and learn of me."

Finding out which is the good way and walking therein, the result is rest for the soul "for I am meek and lowly in heart." I have heard one said, "Knowledge is power," but in this case, knowledge is submission. Submit yourselves therefore to God. Resist the devil, and he will flee from you.

As the NBC morning news theme song saith, "Oh, what a difference today makes." No longer burden down with the troubles of this world as Israel passed over the Jordan River into the promised land. A crossover had taken place. No longer of the old self but a new creation is in control because when Jesus said "But seek you first the kingdom of God and all his righteousness and all these things will be added unto you," he was talking about me, letting me know that this can't be done in one sitting a lifetime of commitment but a full-time obligation. It has a twofold purpose.

The kingdom of heaven is like unto leaven; you don't get it all in one sitting. We got to keep on raising just as physical food needed daily for the natural body so does spiritual when we say "Give us this day our daily bread." It is not just about food for the stomach but that for the soul also. I have heard one said, "If all time is spent in the dos of the Lord, there won't be any time left for the don'ts." He said, "Enter ye in at the straight gates for wide is the gate and broad is the way that leadeth to destruction and many there be which go in there at." I have heard the saying, "You is of a one tract mind," but as long as it is tracking to Jesus, everything is still alright for we are living in a time when death is just a breath away, but as long as Jesus is in control of that breath, everything is still alright. As Paul said, "To be absent from the body is to be present with the Lord."

About the Author

Geneva S. Rivers is a woman of God and of strong faith. Geneva was called into the ministry by God in 1988, and she became an ordained minister in 1990. She believes in speaking what the Lord says. She believes God's word, and her prayer is that all will seek God, repent their sins, and give their lives to Jesus.